The Yankee Pioneers

Happy is the man who recalls his ancestors with pride, who treasures the story of their greatness, tells the tales of their heroic lives, and with joy too full for speech, realizes that fate has linked him with a race of goodly men.

—Goethe

Dedicated to my dear wife
Helen
without whose constant help
during seven years
this book would not have been possible

Samuel B. Pettengill

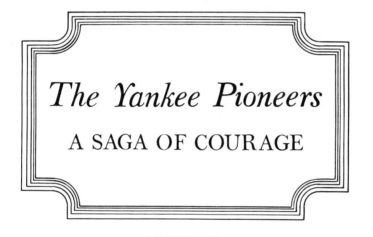

The Yankee Pioneers

A SAGA OF COURAGE

Abridged Paperback Edition

Regional Center for Educational Training

Hanover, New Hampshire

1977

This abridged paperback edition is published by the Regional Center for Educational Training as a title in the Bicentennial Historiettes Series of the Vermont-New Hampshire Bicentennial Educational Resources. All rights reserved.

Publication of this edition has been made possible by grants in aid from the Vermont Bicentennial Commission, the Windham Foundation, and Mrs. Samuel B. Pettengill-and through the courtesy of the publisher, the Charles E. Tuttle Co., Rutland, Vermont 05701, from whom the complete book may be ordered.

Library of Congress Cataloging in Publication Data

77-10753

ISBN 0-915892-11-1

Printed in the United States of America by Fox Publishing Corp.

From the PREFACE to the original Edition:

I HAVE SPOKEN before audiences in forty-four states. In introducing me the chairman has generally said that I had been brought up in Vermont, and that my ancestors had lived there and in New Hampshire and Massachusetts since about 1640 when the first Pettengill came to Salem from England. When the meeting broke up it was almost certain that some persons in the audience would come up to shake my hand and say with pride that they, too, traced back to New England. This convinced me that people still admire the sheer courage and grit of the brave men and women who conquered the New England wilderness.

This book was written as a tribute to one of those pioneers, my great-grandfather Peter, who was born in New Hampshire before the American Revolution. In 1787, when he was eighteen years old, he walked over a hundred miles at the shoulders of a team of oxen to settle in what was then a wilderness and become a citizen of Vermont.

I have attempted to incorporate in this book as much detail about the daily lives of such pioneers as I have been able to find. So much of what went on in those early days was taken for granted that little was written about it, and today what was once common knowledge has been largely forgotten. For instance, when the pioneers first came to the wilderness there was no grass. When I read this in an old diary I was amazed until I walked through the woods near my home and found—no grass.

This made me wonder what else happened that we do not think about today. And the idea of this book was born—to gather all the bits and pieces of information I could find and put them together to make a picture of how our pioneer ancestors lived when they first came to the wilderness. It is the story, not of just one man or one family, but of many who settled in different parts of New England. Despite different problems, all these men and families had one common denominator—courage to face up to their problems.

It is important to remember that with the exception of the power of gun powder and that of river water harnessed in mill dams, the immense task of settling the wilderness was done by only the muscle power of men, women, children, oxen and horses. Steam engines did not come into use in America until after 1800. Decades were to pass before gasoline, fuel oil, natural gas and electricity did all the hard work of the American people.

It would make too long a list to name all the books, records, diaries, letters and other documents I read over a period of more than five years to collect my facts. So at this point I want to thank all the men and women, living and dead, whose writings have been of such great help to me in ferreting out the past.

Seven of the illustrations in the book were selected from a collection of historical drawings owned by the National Life Insurance Co., of Vermont, who generously gave me permission to use them. Drawn from studies of Vermont history by two artists, the late Roy F. Heinrich and the late Herbert Morton Stoops, they show costumes, episodes and backgrounds in accurate accord with the past.

<table>
<tr><td>Grafton, Vermont
1971</td><td>Samuel B. Pettengill</td></tr>
</table>

In Acknowledgment and Appreciation

Publication of this abridged paperback version of *The Yankee Pioneers* has been a considerable challenge - and an even greater privilege.

The challenge was to reduce the word count of the original text while preserving a full measure of its substance and flavor. In order to produce a paperback inexpensive enough to be bought and read by many persons, we had to cut by at least 50 percent. But we also wanted to retain all of author Pettengill's fascinating insights into the realities of pioneer life on the Northern Frontier. And who would presume to dilute his extraordinarily vigorous writing style and colorful vocabulary?

The final abridgement has omitted a few chapters and melded others. But we believe that this paperback edition contains all of the most important conclusions and lessons of the original text. And 99 percent of its words are the ones that Samuel Pettengill wrote. We thank Laura Bohannon, the experienced children's editor who made the original abridgement, and the many others who have read various drafts and made helpful criticisms and suggestions.

The privilege has been the opportunity to make an unusually valuable addition to our educational resources about old-time Vermont and New Hampshire. During the past five years, the Regional Center for Educational Training has produced a variety of historical resources for the schools, resources which combine historical authenticity with high levels of readability and interest. *The Yankee Pioneers* certainly meets both of these criteria in surpassing measure.

We owe a special debt to Mrs. Samuel B. Pettengill, widow of the author. Sincerely dedicated to the principles her husband expressed in *The Yankee Pioneers* she not only authorized this paperback edition but worked hard and unswervingly to make it a reality.

Sincere thanks also go to the Windham Foundation whose generosity permits sale of the book at a price substantially lower than publication costs, and to the Charles E. Tuttle Company who have graciously permitted this abridgement. Copies of the original hardback edition can be secured from their Rutland, Vermont, office.

Hanover, N.H.   Del Goodwin
July 1977   Regional Center for Educational Training

[1]

Yankee Blood

Let us go back in imagination to the first years spent in the wilderness of New England.

What did the endless forest have to say to those ancestors of ours? And with what voice did it speak?

Imagine a one-room cabin at the edge of a deep forest. The nearest neighbors are one, five, or more miles away. It is night and there is no moon. Winter is approaching and the whispering of the first white flakes can be heard. Some of the flakes are drifting in through cracks in the roof. The big trees are swaying and crackling in a rising wind.

The pioneer family whose name you perhaps bear is sitting around the fireplace. They gather strength from its warmth. But as the flames rise and fall, the shadows of father, mother and children change their shapes in strange ways on the walls around them. The fire is their only light. An old dog mutters and growls in his sleep.

But these are not the only voices. Waking from its daytime sleep, an owl hoots. Although he is known to be harmless, the hoot has an ominous sound. Not far off, a bear barks. He weighs perhaps four hundred and fifty pounds.

Further away, a pack of wolves begin to howl. They are hungry, always hungry. In the crotch of a nearby tree, a coon begins to wail. Then comes the scream of a panther.

Little is said. The father banks the fire with infinite care to make sure, very sure, that it will rekindle when daylight comes. It will be cold in the cabin at daybreak. The water in the bucket will be frozen. As the fireplace embers die down, the room grows dark.

Yankee Blood

Great-grandfather Pettengill came to Grafton, Vermont, in 1787 when he was eighteen years old. He walked the entire distance of over a hundred miles, as he drove a team of oxen. They needed someone at their shoulders to guide them with gee and haw unless they were on a familiar road.

Born seven years before Lexington and Concord Bridge, and the son of a Revolutionary soldier, he could also tell much about the generation before him.

★ ★ ★ ★ ★ ★ ★ ★ ★ ★ ★ ★ ★ ★ ★

I grew up in the same small township which he helped to settle. As a small boy I fished for minnows and dace in the same brook where he could easily catch a big mess of trout. I made hay in the same fields where he once swung a scythe; drove a team of oxen just as he had done; pinched potato bugs to death; slept as he had done on a rope bed in the north bedchamber (the coldest room in the house). In summer I slept on two corn husk mattresses, and in winter between the two.

The only heat in the house was the kitchen stove. To save work, the fireplaces were seldom used, usually only when we had company. In bitter winter weather the fire in the kitchen stove would go out.

The water in the kettle would turn to ice which had to be thawed in the dawn's early light in order to prime the pump in the corner of the room.

3

The Yankee Pioneers

In summer's blinding heat at haying time I mopped my brow in the shade of a great elm that was familiar to great-grandfather as his eighty-eight summers came and went. And in late winter, when cold nights but warmer days caused the sap to run in the "sugar bush," I helped collect the thin sweet liquid from the wooden buckets we had earlier hung on the maple trees after tapping them and inserting wooden spouts. It took forty gallons of sap to make one gallon of syrup then, just as it does now, and still more boiling down to make maple sugar. But the results were worth the effort. Is there anything better than maple syrup on hot pancakes on a cold winter morning?

How could the first pioneers manage without matches, butter, vitamins, rubber footwear, bathtubs, electric milking machines, gasoline powered saws, horseless wagons, R.F.D., telephones, super-markets, beauty shops, television, hospitals, drug stores, sleeping pills, headache remedies and electric tooth brushes?

And did the "young-uns" feel abused because they had to sleep on corn husk mattresses and help with the chores?

Jo Ann Stover

Gathering the maple sap.

[2]

Endless Forest, But No Grass

New England was settled from the sea and the early settlers lived close to it and by it. For their food and livelihood they depended chiefly on the sea: building, outfitting and repairing ships, deep sea fishing, shell fishing, whaling, sealing, the evaporation of salt water to produce salt, the making of lime from clam shells and imports to and from the Old World, the West Indies, the East Indies and faraway China.

Beyond the coast country was the great forest. It is not possible for the present generation to visualize its immense sweep and height. The forest was thousands of years old and covered New England, especially the northern part, like a dark blanket. Because the red men had neither axe nor saw, nor anything of iron, they had hardly touched it.

The prime tools for forest land were the axe to cut and the plow to plant as soon as the axe had done its work.

The forest and the man-created clearings in it called for lumbermen and farmers, far different callings from those of the men and women who chiefly lived by, on, and from the sea.

No one can begin to appreciate the gigantic task which confronted the pioneers unless able to visualize the endless and often impenetrable forest. Blot from your eyes the open vistas of today and try to see only what the pioneers saw with the eyes of discovery.

Except in the northernmost counties of Maine, New Hampshire and Vermont, there are today few stretches of highway which are solidly bordered with trees on both sides of the road for more than four or five miles. In 1750 a pioneer could tramp from Massachusetts to Canada in practically unbroken forest.

There were of course a few vistas in the olden time, ponds, lakes, beaver swamps, granite hill tops with too little soil for trees to root in, and fire burns. In 1752 a fire burned for over fifty miles from the White Mountains to the Atlantic coast. Hurricanes or blow downs occasionally leveled a mountainside.

7

There were also a few square miles along river banks where Indians had girdled and killed trees with their stone axes and thus made a little space where corn and pumpkins could grow in the sunlight. Except for these bits of open land, it was a wilderness of trees.

It was in fact, the forest primeval that had covered the land since the end of the glacial period, two hundred centuries ago. It was a place where men used few words and spoke in low tones. Many eyes might be watching, many ears listening. And as birds sing in the sunlight but are hushed in the shade, it seems probable that the stillness of the great forest had something to do with the taciturnity of Yankee speech.

It was endless. It is an old saying that when the Pilgrims landed, a squirrel could go all the way from Plymouth Rock to the Mississippi River without touching ground, eating nuts as he leaped from one tree to the next.

The greatest of the maples, elms, hemlocks, oaks and ash trees grew to be from one hundred to two hundred feet high. An elm in Dunstable, New Hampshire, that was cut down in 1736, when George Washington was four years old, had a diameter of seven feet, eight inches. This would give a circumference of about twenty-four feet.

Endless Forest, But No Grass

Eleazar Wheelock, who founded Dartmouth College in 1769, said that trees grew two hundred feet high on the present campus, and "in one instance, by actual measurement, one tree was found to be two hundred and seventy feet long," which is about the height of a twenty-story building.

Not many church steeples in New England are much more than one hundred feet high. So when you go to church next Sunday, imagine that where the steeple now stands, a tree may have stood that was twice as high as the steeple.

It would be a splendid thing if the good people of every New England town were to locate their oldest tree and then protect it as a living historian of days long gone. School boys and girls would be a little prouder of their towns if this were done.

★ ★ ★ ★ ★ ★ ★ ★ ★ ★ ★ ★ ★ ★ ★

The greatest obstacles that faced the pioneers were neither the Indians nor the cold winters.

One great obstacle was the never ending forest just described. A second great obstacle was the absence of grass.

Without grass or hay there could be no cows, milk, oxen, sheep or horses. The green leaf is a power plant for all living things, the mightiest converter of the sun's energy in the world. Grass is the magic carpet upon which all humanity rides.

Later on we shall see how for lack of grass (hay) Seth Hubbell's ox gave out. He starved to death. Without oxen the pioneers were pack animals, unable to plow, harrow or haul heavy loads. They could not bring their heavy tools such as grindstones and anvils, but only small tools such as axes and augers carried on their backs.

There was some wild grass here and there, but its value as food for cattle was practically nil. It grew on the sides of rivers where the sun could warm a bit of soil a few hours a day, or on the shores of ponds and lakes, or on the edge of wet beaver marshes where the beavers had gnawed down the trees, or along granite ridges on the hill tops. The wild grass grew where a forest fire, started perhaps by lightning, had killed square miles of trees, or where a hurricane's scythe had mowed them down, as in 1938. Pioneers called it browse, a mixture of wild grass, leaves, twigs, sedge, ferns and small brush.

Out of Vermont's nine thousand square miles of land area it is doubtful that there were more than a hundred, and maybe no more than fifty square miles of browse when the white men came. And browse is starvation food.

But how about deer and moose? What did they eat? They lived in the wilderness forests for centuries without grassy meadows and pastures. Why couldn't cattle do the same? One answer is that many deer do perish during the winter from cold and the lack of nourishing food. But most survive. All animals adjust to their environment or die. The Algonquin Indians' name for moose was "twig eater." Moose live on twigs, bark, lily pads, etc. Moose and deer are apt to kill young trees by gnawing off their bark for winter food. There are instances when starving pioneers themselves gnawed the bark of trees.

If you call Indian corn a grass, as a botanist might do, it constitutes a small exception to the general statement about the lack of grass. For example, there were the *Great Meadows* at what is now Newbury, Vermont, and Haverhill, New Hampshire. Here was a wide valley with ox-bow turns in the slow flowing Connecticut. There were probably less than three square miles of what we now call meadows in the ox-bow flats. From time to time, perhaps for centuries, wandering Indian tribes had developed on these flats some rudimentary agriculture such as Indian corn and pumpkins.

Either by girdling or by fire they had killed enough trees to clear about one thousand acres, less than two of the nine thousand square miles in Vermont. Some native grass must have come up with the corn and the pumpkins, but the Indians had no cattle or horses to feed it to.

To replace native browse, settlers planted "English grass." The name of one of our favorite grasses, timothy, comes from Timothy Hanson, born near Keene, New Hampshire, in 1707. He went to Europe and brought back the first timothy grass seed sown in America. He wanted a "croppe that he could sew [sow]."

11

The Yankee Pioneers

In the 1770s there was a favorite "Forefathers' Song":

> The place where we live is a
> wilderness wood
> Where grass is much lacking
> that's fruitful and good.
> Our mountains and hills and
> the valleys below
> Being commonly covered with
> ice and with snow.

Allianora Rosse

[3]

Soldier of the Revolution

Very few of the first settlers in New England left a personal, detailed record of the hardships they endured. One who did was Seth Hubbell, who with his wife and small children settled in what is now Wolcott, Lamoille County, Vermont, about thirty-one miles from the Canadian line.

He started his long journey from Connecticut late in February, 1789. It is apparent that he had spent the previous summer alone in the wilderness, to start clearing and to begin a cabin. He was then in the prime of life, thirty years old.

13

Seth Hubbell was with General Washington at Valley Forge and continued in the service of his country to witness the surrender of Cornwallis at Yorktown in 1781. He then lived in Norwalk, Connecticut, until he decided to make a "pitch" in the new Republic of Vermont where he spent the rest of his life.

In 1824, when he was sixty-five years old, Seth Hubbell did write a narrative of the struggles and hardships he and his wife had endured. It is probable that Hubbell was poorer in tools and equipment than others who later became his neighbors and suffered more hardships than other pioneers with more oxen and tools.

I quote only a part of the memoirs he wrote.
★ ★ ★ ★ ★ ★ ★ ★ ★ ★ ★ ★ ★ ★ ★

In the latter part of February, 1789, I set out from the town of Norwalk, in Connecticut, on my journey for Wolcott, to commence a settlement and make that my residence; family consisting of my wife and five children, they all being girls, the eldest nine or ten years old. My team was a yoke of oxen and a horse.

After I had proceeded on my journey to within one hundred miles of Wolcott, one of my oxen failed [became exhausted], but I however kept him yoked with the other till about noon each day; then took his end of the yoke myself and proceeded on in that manner with my load to about fourteen

Helping the failing ox.

miles of my journey's end, when I could get the sick ox no further, and was forced to leave him with Thomas W. Connel, in Johnson; but he had neither hay nor grain for him.

It was now about the 20th of March; the snow not far from four feet deep; no hay to be had for my team, and no way for them to subsist but by browse [twigs or brush]. As my sick ox at Connel's could not be kept on browse, I interceded with a man in Cambridge for a little hay to keep him alive, which I backed, a bundle at a time, five miles for about ten days, when the ox died. We still had eight miles to travel on snowshoes, by marked trails—no road being cut.

Esq. Taylor, with his wife and two small children, who moved on with me, were the first families in Wolcott. To the east of us it was eighteen miles to inhabitants, and no road but marked trees.

I had now got to the end of my journey. I had not a mouthful of meat or kernel of grain for my family, nor had I a cent of money to buy with, or property that I could apply to that purpose. I however had the good luck to catch a sable. The skin I carried fifty miles, and exchanged for half a bushel of wheat and backed it home . . . .

We had now lived three weeks without bread; though in the time I had bought a moose of an Indian, and backed the meat five miles, which answered to subsist on. No grain or provision of any kind, of consequence, was to be had on the river Lamoille. I had to go into New Hampshire, sixty miles, for the little I had for my family till harvest. The three remaining children that I left in Hyde Park [distance nine miles], I brought, one at a time, on my back on snowshoes, as also the whole of my goods . . . .

I moved from Connecticut with the expectation of having fifty acres of land given me, but this I was disappointed of, and under the necessity of selling a yoke of oxen [apparently Hubbell had acquired an ox to take the place of the one that died] and a horse to buy the land I now live on, which reduced my stock to one cow, and this I had the misfortune to lose the next winter. That left me wholly destitute of a single hoof of a creature, and the next summer I had to support my family without a cow.

In the fall I had the good fortune to purchase another cow, but my misfortunes still continued, for in the June following she was killed by a singular accident. Again I was left without a cow.

When I first came into Wolcott, my farming tools consisted on one axe and an old hoe. The first year I cleared about two acres, wholly without any team. When too faint to labor, for want of food, I used to take a fish from the river, broil it on the

17

coals and eat it without bread or salt, and then to my work again. This was my common practice the first year till harvest. I could not get a single potato to plant the first season, so scarce was this article. I planted the land which I cleared in season with corn, and an early frost ruined the crop. My seed corn I had to go twenty miles after . . . .

In the course of the winter I was so fortunate as to catch sable enough to pay my debts. I had now gone to the extent of my ability for bread-corn, but was destitute of meat. I had to have recourse to wild meat for a substitute and had the good luck to purchase a moose of a hunter; and the meat of two more I brought in on shares—had the one for bringing in the other. These two were uncommonly large, were judged to weigh seven hundred weight each. The meat of these three moose I brought in on my back, together with the large bones and heads. I backed them five or six miles over rough land, cut up by sharp ridges and deep hollows, and interspersed with underbrush and windfalls, which made it impracticable to pass with a hand sled, which could I have used, would have much eased my labor.

Those who are acquainted with this kind of burden may form an idea of the great difficulty of carrying a load on snowshoes in the time of a thaw. It is wearisome at such times to travel without a load; but with one, especially at this late season, it is intolerable, but thaw or freeze, my necessities obliged me to be at my task, and still to keep up my burthen.I had to draw my fire-wood through the winter on a hand sled; in fact, my snowshoes were constantly hung to my feet;

★ ★ ★ ★ ★ ★ ★ ★ ★ ★ ★ ★ ★ ★ ★

Seth Hubbell died in 1832 at the age of seventy-three, leaving his "rich, beautiful farm to his sons." Some readers may think that Hubbell was the victim of his own folly in starting his long journey in February. It is, however, probable that he wanted to start while there was still snow on the ground for his sled to run on, not realizing how much deeper the snow would become as he went north.

It was much easier to move heavy loads in winter on sleds, sledges or stone boats. It was thus that the huge stones in the foundations of houses, barns, bridges and so forth were moved into place in the old days. Any pioneer could make a wooden sledge, whereas axles, spokes and iron-rimmed wheels called for experts. In fact, years later when there were roads of a sort, it was still the custom to move heavy loads on sleds, because wheeled vehicles would bog down in muddy ruts.

Many southern New Englanders were not familiar with Vermont, New Hampshire and Maine winters. Witness a college graduate who, with his family, came to Townshend, Vermont, ten years after Seth Hubbell's journey. They left Uxbridge, Massachusetts, on March 9, 1799, with their household goods mounted on a sled drawn by two yoke of oxen. When they left Uxbridge there were only three inches of snow.

When they reached West Townshend, the snow was six feet deep on the level. It took nineteen yoke of oxen of the neighbors to break out a road and drag the sled up a steep hill to their new home.

One of the family was a fourteen-year-old boy named Peter. It was his assignment to lead the family cow, on foot, the entire distance. As the crow flies, this was not less than ninety miles, and considerably more over hill and dale on foot. The last name of this boy was Taft. Had he lived until March 4, 1909, he would have been very proud to witness an event that took place in Washington, D.C., in which his grandson figured prominently, the inauguration of President William Howard Taft.

[4]

As Others Saw Them

One of the few, and probably the best on-the-spot record of pioneer life in Western New England in the late 1700s is that of the Rev. Nathan Perkins. He was the pastor of the Third Church of West Hartford, Connecticut (Congregational) and held that pastorate for sixty-six years.

In 1789 he made a trip on horseback through western New England. He traveled alone. He left his home on April 17, went as far north as Burlington, Vermont, and returned home on June 11. He was a founder of the Connecticut Missionary Society. This was his main reason for making the arduous trip.

21

I quote briefly from his diary, in his own spelling and old-fashioned use of words. If you read it you will be both saddened and amused.

He visited about forty settlements in Massachusetts and Vermont, spending a day in each, and preaching whenever invited. He went through forty other townships that were uninhabited. "I have made more than a hundred miles and seen no meeting house [north of Bennington]." He preached in log huts, barns, or out of doors, wherever an audience would gather.

Pownal had a "miserable set of inhabitants—Rhode Island haters of religion," Bennington's "people, proud, scornful, conceited." At Sunderland "a raving arminian Methodist preached in ye evening. Here lived formerly ye awful Deist Ethan Allyn, one of the wickedest men y^t ever walked this guilty Globe .... I looked at the grave with pious horror." (Allen had died the previous February.) At Middlebury he found "wretched fare, wretched bed, eat up with fleas, no hay, my horse starving." At Brandon the "meanest of all lodging, dirty, fleas without number."

At New Haven, Vermont, he "preached at a log house—nothing but brook water to drink . . . slept in an open log house where it rained on me in ye night and no keeping [hay and oats] for my horse." At Williston he met Governor Chittenden. "A low, poor house —a low, vulgar man, clownish but made me welcome . . . a shrewd cunning man . . . understands extremely well ye mysteries of Vermont." Chittenden was Vermont's first Governor.

"Moose plenty on ye mountains . . . and wolves plenty . . . no beef, no butter. I pine for home, for my own table . . . . Far absent, among strangers, all alone, log huts, people nasty, low-lived, indelicate, and miserable cooks.

"Mud up to my horse's belly. Night came in, I could travel no farther. I found a little log hut and put up there, could get no supper, my horse no feed, slept on a chaff bed without covering, a man, his wife and three children all in ye same nasty stinking room."

His horse didn't like Vermont any better than he did, for at Essex "my horse got away and steered for Hartford, he had undergone hardships enough, he thought."

Despite the harshness of some of his judgments, the Reverend Perkins tried to be just. In fact he had words of admiration. For example, "Preached on ye Sabbath. A large audience deeply attentive . . . some very clever, serious and sensible. In a few years be a good Country, pleasant and well to live on."

"When I go from hut to hut, ye people nothing to eat, to drink, to wear, yet ye women serene, contented, loving their husbands, wanting never to return, nor any dressy clothes . . . .

"Woods make people love one another and be kind and obliging and good natured. They set much more store by one another than in ye old settlements."

23

This diary makes more credible the harsh difficulties that confronted Seth Hubbell. He and Reverend Perkins must have followed the same wilderness trail much of the way.

Many times in the spring and growing season of the year, the clergyman's horse found little or no grass, no hay, and of course no oats. "My horse was deeply grieved," wrote the clergyman, and "my ox failed," wrote old soldier Seth Hubbell.

from: *Stage-Coach & Tavern Days,* by Alice M. Earle Courtesy, Dover Publications, Inc., New York

[5]

Why They Came, and Lived on Hills

Following the surrender by France in 1763 of all claims to territory east of the Mississippi, the magnetic needle of migration swerved northward and inland. Nearly all the settlers in Maine, New Hampshire and Vermont left homes in Massachusetts, Rhode Island and Connecticut. In fact, Vermont was first officially named "New Connecticut."

Why did the tide of migration turn to the north? Some people think that the settlers were fools to go to hilly, rock-strewn country rather than to the rich, flat and rock-free meadow lands west of the Appalachians.

These critics do not know the economics of transportation. The westward course of empire from New England did not get under way until the construction of the Erie Canal in 1825.

While this explains the logic of northward migration in the late 1700s and early 1800s, it does not tell why the settlers moved at all.

Why did Seth Hubbell and other pioneers go to northern Vermont? There were several reasons that we know of, any one of which might have influenced the settlers.

Although there was plenty of land left in lower New England, nevertheless as it became settled it began to have greater money value. Hence it was logical for the younger generation to think of the practically free land in northern New England as a better place to start their lives. Also there was a continuing heavy demand for lumber of all sorts to export to England and Europe for the "King's Navy," to build ships operating out of the New England seaports, and the winter heating of homes in New England.

For some years the small town of Burlington, Vermont, on Lake Champlain, was the largest lumber exporting town in the United States, the lumber moving by water northward to the St. Lawrence River and thence to the Atlantic Ocean and the world.

Fur trapping was a major occupation in New England for a long time. The skins of the deer, fox, bear, mink, sable, marten, fisher, raccoon and beaver were in great demand. As the forests were cleared in lower New England, the wild animals moved northward and the white men followed.

Another reason Vermont was attractive to settlers from other New England states was its conservative monetary policy. Vermont was officially a separate nation from the time of its own Declaration of Independence on January 17, 1777, until she joined the Union in 1791. She had no part or responsibility, therefore, in the flood of paper money issued by the Continental Congress.

"Not worth a continental" was the reproach attached to the so-called dollars of paper money. By 1781, this currency fell to one thousand for one dollar in hard money. Foreigners bought five thousand dollars worth of Continental scrip for a single dollar of gold.

Uriel Cross came to Vermont from Connecticut with four hundred and eighty-seven dollars in silver which he had saved during three years of hard work. Desiring to join the Green Mountain Boys under Col. Remember Baker, he was advised to exchange his hard (and heavy) money for Continental currency. This he did.

When his army service ended a couple of years later, he had to exchange seventy-two dollars of paper currency for one dollar in silver coin. His original four hundred and eighty-seven dollars in silver had therefore shrunk to about seven dollars. As he bemoaned, "In this way I did worse than to sit down and done nothing."

Old Tom Chittenden, Vermont's first governor, who served for seventeen years and had only one eye, could not see how a government could make its people affluent by printing dollar signs on pieces of paper and making them legal tender! He was a conservative in money matters. Vermont coined its own hard money and did not go head-over-heels in debt. Its legislature decreed that counterfeiters should "suffer death;" nothing less.

This was later softened to forfeiture of the counterfeiter's entire estate, cutting off his right ear, branding him with a hot iron with the letter "C," and imprisoning him for life. This was strong medicine, but it created confidence in the new Republic of Vermont and undoubtedly influenced migration to the state.

The laws of inheritance probably influenced some of the migration to Maine, Vermont and New Hampshire. The old English system of primogeniture and entail of land to the oldest son never got firmly rooted in New England. Nevertheless, the laws of Massachusetts and Connecticut provided that when a man died intestate, his oldest son inherited a double portion of the land, subject of course to the widow's dower. This meant that the oldest son got twice as much land, in value, as each of his younger brothers. Daughters inherited no land if there were sons. These laws of inheritance were bound to make the younger sons and daughters, and the wives of the sons, unhappy with their lot.

The Vermont legislature, on the other hand, as early as 1779, provided that, subject to the widow's dower, the sons and daughters should have "equal portions" in value of the real and personal estate. The sons were to have their portions in land, so far as the property would allow, and the daughters their equal portions in the personal property.

Also, without getting into the merits of one religious creed as against another, it is plain that many young people in the late 1700s were breaking away from the more severe precepts of Calvinism. Infant damnation seemed too extreme to many, and particularly to the younger members of a community. Evidently a substantial rift developed between the older and more church-going folk in Connecticut and the younger generation that was pioneering in Vermont.

The slow trickle of the first settlers northward was turned into a flood by important political events. The most important was the signing of the peace treaty with Great Britain on September 3, 1783. This terminated all authority, whether actual or claimed, by the royal governors of New Hampshire over the landowners of Vermont.

But New York continued to claim title to all Vermont! Her royal governors had issued "grants" to Vermont land, as New Hampshire had done.

Finally, on October 28, 1790, Vermont paid New York thirty thousand dollars to settle her claims to Vermont land. Four months later Vermont was admitted to the Union as the fourteenth state.

With these questions settled, the pioneers considered their land titles to be safe, and poured into Vermont, almost doubling its population in ten years.

Most of the early settlers chose their home sites on the high places instead of in the valleys. Why? The chief reason was that there were more beaver than people in the long-ago days, animals which had the inconsiderate habit of damming up brooks and rivers until the lowlands were an impenetrable marsh. The swarms of mosquitoes, gnats, blowflies and other insects that made life miserable for man and beast were not quite so thick on the hills as in the dank and swampy valleys choked with willows, alders and brush.

It was believed that the chance of escaping malaria, typhoid fever and other crippling diseases was better on the drier hillsides.

Moreover, there were more hours of sunlight on the hills and upland meadows for the growing of crops. The sun shone earlier in the morning and lingered later in the day on the eastern and southern slopes. In effect this lengthened the growing season by several days, an important consideration. And the season's first frost hit the valley farms earlier and harder than the hill farms. In building a house or cabin, it was erected whenever possible so that the rooms most used faced east and south to catch the sunlight. This also helped to save firewood in the winter.

The upland farm had a "view." A view has meant much to people of all races and times. But it meant more to our Yankee forebears, for whom the days were never long enough to do the work that had to be done. They understood the Bible words, "I will lift up mine eyes to the hills from whence cometh my help."

[6]

Pack Animals and Log Cabins

When the Pilgrims landed at Plymouth Rock in 1620, there was not a single ox or horse in what is now New England. It was not until 1624 that three heifers and a bull were brought across the ocean to Plymouth. In short, the Pilgrims had no milk for four years! In 1630, ten years after the landing at Plymouth, there were only three cows in New England. As to horses, there were very few in northern New England until after 1800.

For many years, while cattle and horses were bred, and calves and colts were growing up, the first settlers in the wilderness grants had to depend almost entirely on human muscle. Actually the pioneers were pack

31

animals, with little but strong backs and stout hearts. There was a saying among the pioneers that a man who could not carry a hundred pounds on his back for ten miles was "not fit to begin a new settlement."

A settler in Poultney, Vermont, walked thirty miles to Manchester with one hundred pounds of iron on his back, and returned the next day with one hundred pounds of salt. Colonel Crafts walked from Sturbridge, Massachusetts, to what is now Craftsbury, Vermont, a distance of one hundred and twenty miles. For part of the journey he drew his wife on a hand sled, "there being no road." A Mr. Reed, of Troy, Vermont, on snowshoes, carried a plow on his back for twenty miles.

Deacon Burnap, of Lebanon, Connecticut, having made his pitch near Norwich, Vermont, walked home, assembled his wife and six children, "burdening each according to their several capacities," with the heaviest burden on his own shoulder. The whole family then "footed the entire distance back to Norwich," a distance of one hundred and forty miles as the crow flies, and many more by the twisting trails.

Where were the pioneers going? Almost invariably to a log cabin.

There is no more solid fixture in American folklore than the log cabin. To have been born in one has been a prime political asset to office seekers from constable

Building their wilderness home.

to president. It was therefore painful to me to learn that the log cabin is not an American invention. There was none in what is now New England for twenty years or more after Plymouth Rock.

The red man knew nothing of log cabins. They had no iron and hence no metal axes or saws. Most Indian shelters in New England were wigwams, made by thrusting saplings into the ground in a circle, pulling their tops together in the form of a dome. They were covered with animal hides or bark from elm, birch, or other trees, and then plastered with mud or clay to keep out the rain and snow. White settlers occasionally made temporary shelters similar to wigwams.

The historians seem to agree that the idea of log cabins came over with the Swedes who first settled in Delaware around 1638, some eighteen years after Plymouth Rock. The idea spread like wildfire to New England and elsewhere. A log cabin, however crude, was a sturdy shelter. A good axe-man alone in the forest could make a log cabin without help except for hauling the logs to the selected site and lifting them into place. The only tools absolutely essential were an axe, a whetstone and an auger. The auger bored holes into which wooden tree nails called "trunnels" were driven. Iron nails were not to be had.

The famous Eleazar Wheelock started Dartmouth College in the New Hampshire wilderness by building a "hut" of logs for his family. It was eighteen feet square "without stone, brick, glass or nails." His nearest neighbor was over two miles away. "I see nothing but lofty pines about me," he said.

With the large number of children in those "good old days," the cabins were generally crowded. And sometimes there were other families and friends. A classic case of crowding is that of Jonathan Perham and Ephraim Holden, of Rindge, New Hampshire. In the dead of winter in 1780 they and their families took possession of an abandoned log hut in Athens, Vermont. Shortly after, they were joined by a third family, that of Seth Oakes from Winchendon, Massachusetts. Mrs. Oakes gave birth to a daughter, the first born in the township.

The thirty or forty trees needed to build a small cabin paid three dividends. One was the cabin itself. Another was the clearing made in the forest where the trees had been cut down. The land had to be cleared anyway for the growing crops. Third, the pioneers needed wood to cook their food and to keep warm. The pioneer had all the wood he could burn. Nothing gave him greater happiness than a roaring fire. In this respect, at least, he need skimp no more.

[7]

Light and Heat

The flint missed fire. The gun did not shoot. The owner of the gun died—perhaps from the claws of a bear, or the return fire of an Indian, as did the famous Remember Baker, Ethan Allen's close relative. The flintlock musket of the pioneers depended upon a spark ignited by the friction of steel on flint as the trigger was pulled. The spark had to reach the priming powder in the flash pan before it expired a second later. Hence the name "firearm" and the expression "hold your fire."

But the chief need of a pioneer family was heat and light, and a method similar to that of the musket was used. Holding a flint in the left hand and striking it sharply downward with a piece of iron or steel, one could hope that a spark would fall into the tinder box

36

and ignite. The tinder had to be a very dry, inflammable substance such as partially charred linen cloth. Under the best of circumstances striking a fire was a painstaking job.

Vermont's famous judge, Wendell Phillips Stafford, in his address on Ann Story, spoke of "the settler crouching by his hearth where the last faint ember has expired, trying with infinite pains to bring the birth of fire from the cold marriage of flint and steel." One historian of colonial days wrote that she had struck flint with steel hundreds of times without success. Charles Dickens, who visited the United States in 1857, said that with luck he could strike fire in a half hour or so. Hence the expression "strike a light."

Suppose the room was below zero and snow driven through the roof and walls of the log cabin had made everything damp? Or that the flint was lost? Or that there was no dry wood?

It was very important when they banked the fire for the night to cover some of the live embers with ashes. Cut off from much of the oxygen, the embers could be expected to keep "alive" until morning when they could be uncovered and blown into a blazing fire. If the embers died during the night, or the family went away for several days, it was necessary to again resort to flint and steel, or send someone to the nearest neighbor to borrow some live coals and bring them back in a fire "scoop." If the nearest neighbor was miles away, and the snow lay three feet deep, the pioneer family had a real problem, especially if it was zero weather. Sometimes pioneers froze to death.

Boy Scouts know there is another way to start a fire which was used by the Indians. That is to use the friction of a rapidly revolving dry stick of wood, one end resting in a hole in another piece of wood. The point of contact of the two pieces can get hot enough to start a flame. I have found no mention of any pioneer using this method, but do not doubt that it was used when flint and steel were missing.

Apart from sunlight, firelight was the only light the pioneers had when they first settled in the wilderness. They went to bed at dark and got up at dawn. Later on light was produced in the cabins by burning torches made of pitch pine, or the pith of dried rushes soaked in grease. A grease-soaked rush or rag was used in a "betty lamp," a small container usually made of iron, with a vertical handle.

Candles came next, made by tying wicks of hemp, tow or silk down from milkweed to a wand and dipping them in hot wax until the desired thickness was reached. Animal fats were used, but they were unpleasant to smell and gave a poor light. Wax from a beehive or from bayberries made the best candles.

Providing plenty of dry wood was one of the most demanding jobs of the settlement. Windfall trees, or standing but dead trees, were selected for cutting when available as they were at least partly free from sap.

They were then "snaked" from the woods by oxen. They were cut into fireplace length, split when necessary and kept under cover if possible. A shed or roof over the wood was almost as important as the wood itself. If there were no shed, the firewood could be piled in a long row and covered with bark to keep off the snow and the rain as much as possible.

To heat a cabin all winter and to cook and wash dishes and clothes all year required fifteen to twenty cords of wood. If cut and piled in a single row, in cordwood width, length and height, the wood pile would be one hundred and twenty to one hundred and sixty feet long.

[8]

Honey Bees

When the white men came to New England in 1620 there were no honey bees, just as there were no cows, sheep, oxen, or horses. Forest trees can live for centuries without honey bees. But there are very few meadow and orchard crops, such as clover and apples, that can reproduce themselves on a large scale without honey bees.

Only a relatively few plants are self-pollinating. Most depend on cross-pollination by wind, birds, or burrs attaching themselves to the family dog or other animals. Chiefly, however, cross-pollination is done by

40

insects which of course include wasps, hornets and yellow jackets. Some eighty per cent of the insects visiting an orchard or meadow today are honey bees.

Only eighteen years after Plymouth Rock honey bees began to be imported from the Old World to New England. The Indians had never seen them and called them "white men's flies." They multiplied very fast and apparently kept a little ahead of the pioneers as they moved into the great forest.

It must have been a great comfort to the settler and his hard-working wife to have ten or twenty thousand or more "farm hands" working for them without charge! To keep the bees, or new swarms of them, from hiving in hollow trees where they were hard to get at, they were often provided with a home called a "skep," or hive made of tightly braided straw in the shape of an upside-down basket. When cold weather came, they were put under cover.

When I was a boy, we put the hives in the attic over the woodshed. There they had some protection from the bitter cold. They were kept dry, with plenty to eat. All winter long I liked to go up near the hives and listen to the never ending musical hum of the busy little people. And what a delight it must have been to the pioneer's wife way back in the old days, when a lilac slip which she had carried from her former home "down country," brought forth its first blossom at the cabin door, and on it a busy honey bee! It was a sign of better times to come.

The pioneers were kind to honey bees. They could not have known what scientific men know today—that the bees that produce one pound of honey for you to enjoy have flown a distance of once or twice around the world. New England folklore tells us that in an Indian raid against a white man's village, they knocked over a beehive. This made the bees very angry and the Indians very scarce.

[9]

Wild Animals and Passenger Pigeons

Amos Story was one of the first settlers of Salisbury, Vermont. He said that he and his fellow pioneers could not have survived if it had not been for the wild animals. The pioneers had to be flesh eaters to survive. A few kinds of wild vegetable life were edible, but fish, birds, and quadrupeds were the indispensable and only food in the long winter months.

The famous Major Robert Rogers of the "Rangers" and some friendly Indians filled a bark canoe with salmon in about half an hour. They used no hooks or nets; one Indian held a lighted pine torch to attract the fish to the side of the canoe where another Indian speared them.

43

In Brownington, Vermont, four men caught "five hundred pounds of dressed trout in one day." A pond near a pioneer settlement was often called "our meat barrel," so full was it of fish.

Fishing in the Connecticut River just below Bellows Falls and North Walpole was so good that settlers on both sides of the river neglected agriculture for many years. They fished not only for their own use but as a business to supply markets down river. But there was scarcely a river in New Hampshire or Vermont that emptied into the Connecticut or Lake Champlain or the Atlantic Ocean that was not good for salmon fishing during the spawning season in the old days when salmon weighing up to twenty pounds could be caught in large numbers.

The Great Falls were, however, too much for the shad that also came up from salt water to spawn. Shad were so thick below the falls during the spawning season that "they could be caught by hand."

Lake Champlain was full of lake trout, salmon, sturgeon and pike that were caught both summer and winter. And speckled trout were in every stream.

As the unpolluted waters jumped with fish, the forest teemed with birds and quadrupeds.

There were wolves, moose, deer, bears, panthers or "catamounts," partridges as thick as barnyard hens, wild turkeys, pigeons, eagles, wild cats or lynx, beavers, muskrats, foxes, raccoons, porcupines, skunks, wood-chucks, martens, rabbits, weasels, mink, otter, squirrels and many others. Nearly all of these in one way or another contributed to the food, clothing, floor and bed coverings of the pioneers. The hides often took the place of money at the trading posts and early stores.

The moose was the largest of the animals, sometimes seven feet tall, weighing up to thirteen hundred pounds and with horns spreading eight feet from tip to tip. Deer were everywhere and became something of a pest when crops began to be grown. But they more than paid their way with venison and hides for clothing, shoes and hats.

We now come to bears. A pioneer log cabin belonging to Thomas Davis in Grafton, Vermont, had an opening for a door, but no door, only an old bed quilt where the door was supposed to be. The wife pestered her husband for months to build a strong, solid door, but without result; he was too busy with more important work, he thought.

Later when the good wife was alone, knitting, and the cabin was filled with the fragrance of supper, a big bear poked his nose through the door. The wife screamed and probably threw hot water at the bear, which fled. All other operations ceased completely until a solid door filled the opening.

Bears destroyed growing corn and garden crops. They relished honey, calves and little pigs. One night when her husband was away, a Mrs. Graves of Brook-field, Vermont, heard loud noises in the pig pen and found a bear trying to get at their swine. She seized a pitchfork, climbed on top of the pig pen and thrust the fork at the bear whenever he got near the squealing pigs. She and the bear kept this up all night. Every pig was saved.

Wolves had no assets whatever. They were not valued for either flesh or fur, and they made it almost impossible to raise sheep. From the beginning bounties were paid for killing them, and they were practically eradicated by the time pioneering ended.

The most feared wild animal was the panther or catamount. His scream made blood run cold. It was like that of a completely terrified woman. Actually the panther's image was worse than the animal. We are told in the *Field Guide to American Wild Life* that "there are no authentic records that this large, shy cat has ever made an unprovoked attack on a human being." But the pioneers in the Vermont and New Hampshire wilderness in the late 1700s never read this book. Nor would they believe it if they had. The catamount was a powerful animal and as quick as lightning. One old record tells us that a panther "took a large calf out of a pen, where the fence was four feet high, and carried it off. With this load it ascended a ledge of rock where one of its leaps was fifteen feet in height. After being shot and hit twice, its fury did not cease but with the last remains of life."

The panther's small cousin is the wildcat or Canadian lynx. When one is alone in the woods at dusk, without a gun or even a stick, it is no fun to look a wildcat in the eye. I know; I did it once.

A hungry bear.

And now comes the most lovable wild animal of them all, then and now, the beaver.

In Williams's *History of Vermont* [1809] there is a charming description of the home life of these busy little citizens who peopled the wilderness long before the red or white man came. I quote briefly:

In September, the happy couple lay up their store of provisions for winter. This consists of bark, the tender twigs of trees and various kinds of soft wood. When their provisions are prepared, the season of love and repose commences.

During the winter they remain in their cabins, enjoying the fruits of their labor and partaking of the sweets of domestic happiness . . . . If any injury is done to their public works, the whole society are soon collected, and join all their forces to repair the injury which affects their commonwealth.

Nothing can exceed the peace and regularity which prevails in the families and throughout their commonwealth. No discord or contention ever appears in any of their families. There is no pilfering or robbing from one another . . . . Different societies of beavers never make war upon one another, or upon any other animals.

What an example to mankind! No crimes, wars, divorces, beggars or drunks!

Wild Animals and Passenger Pigeons

There were game birds such as wild turkeys, geese and ducks, not to mention some of the songbirds of today. Flocks of pigeons, however, were so numerous as to darken the sky and break down the branches of trees from their sheer weight when they roosted at night. Acres of land under groves of beech trees were covered with their dung.

In the spring as they flew by the millions from the Florida Everglades as far north as Hudson Bay and Nova Scotia and west to Mississippi and beyond, they looked like a cloud of giant locusts circling in dark masses twenty miles wide. Early settlers wrote of pigeons' nesting grounds ten miles wide and eighty miles long, with every tree and bush laden with nests.

Audubon in 1842 saw a single flock outside of New England which he estimated to contain over one billion birds, and which he calculated covered an area one hundred and eighty miles long. He figured this one flock would eat eight million bushels of food in a single day. They were usually described as voracious and greedy and the damage they did on cultivated land can scarcely be imagined.

During the height of passenger pigeon migrations, farmers would stop work to kill them by the thousands as they passed overhead. But gunpowder was expensive and most hunters, especially those who supplied the markets where the squabs were in great demand, used nets and traps.

It has been estimated that in the early 1800s, forty per cent of the bird population in the United States was passenger pigeons, and it seemed inconceivable that they would ever disappear. Yet their wanton slaughter over the years was such that within a hundred years the last wild pigeon was killed. On March 24, 1900, a little boy with a BB gun shot it in an oak grove in Pike County, Ohio. One passenger pigeon which had been trapped in 1885 was still living at that time in the Cincinnati Zoological Gardens Zoo. The average life of a passenger pigeon was less than ten years. But "old Martha" lived to the incredible age of twenty-nine, dying in 1914. It was almost as if, the last of her kind, she refused to die.

[10]

Snakes and Insects

Among the seldom mentioned hazards of pioneer days were rattlesnakes and insects.

Around Bennington, Vermont, rattlesnakes were so numerous that the first town meeting voted to pay a bounty for each snake killed. In some areas of Windsor County, Vermont, rattlesnakes were so thick that farm hands refused to go there to work.

Fall Mountain, opposite Bellows Falls on the Connecticut River, was a favorite habitat of the reptiles as they like rocky ridges with sunny exposures. They have gradually been killed off by men, by fires that swept over the mountain and by hogs which attacked and killed them at sight.

51

Rattlesnakes were not entirely useless to the pioneers, however. Some of them valued "rattlesnake oil" for medicinal purposes. Indians used their skins as belts to hold up their loincloths.

From time immemorial housewives have been battling insects of various kinds inside their homes—mosquitoes, flies, fleas, ants, cockroaches and bedbugs. Think what it was like when there were no such things as window or door screens, or even mosquito netting, much less the various death-dealing sprays now found in every supermarket.

Thousands of insects are destructive of crops, fruit trees, farm animals and the health and life of men and women. Yet the books on the old days in Yankee-land have only a few pages on the lifelong struggle of the pioneers against destructive insects.

To cut down an acre or two of primeval forest and let the sun shine on ground which had not felt its direct warmth for centuries; to "toe in" the first planting of the precious seed of corn or wheat and then watch the growing crop chewed up by insects against which they had no adequate defenses was a heartbreaking ordeal.

In 1770 Eleazar Wheelock, president of Dartmouth College, wrote, "brown worms [caterpillars] four inches long attacked the crops; covered the ground—ten bushels of worms raked into a pile, blanketed the house inside and out." Timothy Dwight wrote that grasshoppers in Bennington, Vermont, ate the silk off growing corn and killed the crop. He also recorded that the Hessian fly was a serious pest to growing wheat. And after the wheat was in the barn, it then had to face the weevils.

The larvae of the codling moth fed on apple and other fruit trees. In addition to grain, weevils infested nuts and the bark of trees. The gypsy moth, chinch bug, potato beetle, termite ants and many another insect ate their fill on what the settlers had worked twelve-hour days to raise. Other insects attached themselves to cattle, horses and sheep—parasites such as the screw worm, botfly, lice and fleas, always reducing the animals' vitality and in time killing them.

The common housefly is worldwide and was probably the worst offender of all. It breeds in barn manure and outdoor privies. As barns and barnyards were usually near the house, and sometimes under the same roof, flies polluted human food and helped spread anthrax, Asiatic cholera and the bubonic plague. Mosquitoes were largely responsible for typhoid fever and malaria. Then there were bedbugs, lice and ants.

Even when insects did no direct harm to men or beasts, they exhausted their energy in fighting them off and in loss of sleep. Unless one covered his head with a blanket, the only partial protection from mosquitoes was smoke.

No wonder the pioneers welcomed the return of cold weather. Harvest time was the happiest season of the year, not only because husbands and wives and the children could see what they had accomplished, but because they could sleep soundly at night. The foregoing is not a pleasant tale, but it has to be told for us today to understand a little of what pioneer life really was, and the courage of those who lived it.

The pioneers had other allies such as the insect-eating birds.

Did you ever see a mother hen chasing a grasshopper with her little chicks running after her? Or a toad making a meal of insects? Or a trout leaping in a brook for a bug? There are dozens of species of flycatching birds that live chiefly on insects, among which is the Red-eyed Vireo which was once the most abundant bird in North America.

Modern insecticides, wisely used, have been a great blessing. But before they emerged from the laboratories, the age-old balance of nature often did yeoman work for the pioneers.

[11]

No Salt, but Much Potash

To the chapter "No Grass" we add "No Salt." By that we mean rock salt—sodium chloride such as is found today on every kitchen table in America and in thousands of barns and pasture lots.

You may say, "But surely there were salt licks where pools of brackish water had evaporated on the surface of the ground and left a sediment that could be licked up by wild and domestic animals." The only salt lick I have found mentioned was at Bridport, Vermont. But it was not sodium chloride. It was sulphate of magnesia, which is a purgative known as Epsom Salts.

Fishermen on the seacoast of what is now New England had a large foreign trade with Europe and the West Indies. That trade consisted chiefly of salt water fish, cod, halibut and salmon, and furs of all kinds, which required huge quantities of salt to keep the fish edible and to cure the hides, pelts and skins of beavers, deer, moose, bears, martens, sables, foxes, etc. Without salt there would have been no foreign trade in fish and furs and the settlement of New England would have been postponed for many years.

Fortunately, the same ships that carried fish and furs to markets overseas returned loaded with salt. This solved the problem for New England's seacoast towns. It was, however, another matter for the pioneers who chose the forest and not the sea. They had to have a brine barrel also for salt pork and pickles, salt for butter and hams. They also had to cure the hides of animals to make leather for boots, britches, harness, snowshoes and dozens of other articles.

The settlers' cattle were fond of salt and if they could lick a cake of salt at home they seldom wandered far. In the absence of salt they were apt to wander miles from home, and the time spent in the search for them was a great aggravation to the pioneers.

The transportation of imported salt from the seacoast towns to the homes on the hills was a costly operation. Salt is heavy; it must be kept dry and needs tight containers. Salt was an expensive necessity.

No Salt but Much Potash

Jonathan Dike, of Chittenden, Vermont, brought a bushel of salt from Bennington, a distance of about sixty miles, and was offered a bushel of corn for each pint of salt. On a volume basis this put the value of salt at about sixty-four times that of corn. Salt was at all times scarce and at no time available to the pioneers except at prices which were almost prohibitive.

It might be asked why the early settlers did not get salt from the Atlantic Ocean which was right at their door. The settlers did try to do so many times, but without success. The ocean is about three per cent salt, which means that it took about three hundred and fifty gallons of sea water to produce a bushel of salt. The salt can be separated only by evaporation by the heat of the sun, which costs nothing, or by burning fuel, which is expensive. Huge pans or vats must be used with protection from rainfall. All such efforts ended in financial failure.

If salt for table use and cattle was scarce and expensive on the frontier, the pioneers had a plentiful and valuable supply of another kind of salt, the *lye salts* that were also called potash.

The first settlers in the up-country towns of New England had potash works that served them well for a couple of generations and then, when it seemed to be a permanent source of income, it vanished.

As the forest trees were cut down, most of those not used for log cabins and fuel were burned to ashes. This helped to get rid of the tree trunks and branches so that crops could be planted. There were huge quantities of ashes as the trees were cut down and burned. For days on end in spring and summer, the atmosphere was filled and the sun obscured by smoke.

The ashes were valuable in themselves. They were collected and slowly leached with water, which produced a dark liquid called lye, or potassium carbonate, a strong alkali. The lye was then poured into huge iron pots at the works and the water in the lye was boiled out, leaving a grey, dry, friable anhydrous powder or crystals called potash, or pearl ash. The word potash came from the huge iron pots in which the lye was boiled dry.

In nearly every town with a dozen families or more, there was a potash works. This made it possible for a number of pioneers to co-operate in leaching the lye from its ashes and boiling the water out of the lye to produce the potash. The huge, heavy iron pots were often beyond the financial means of a single family, being much bigger than the household iron pots in which much of the cooking was done.

When I was a boy, the "works" were long since gone, but many a farm home, as late as 1910, had a barrel of ashes under the eaves that caught rain water to leach their own lye, just as their great-grandfathers and mothers had done. They boiled the lye with hog fats and kitchen greases and produced a thick liquid soft soap. By further boiling, it became hard soap which was cut into cakes like today's "store" soap. After washing one's hands with this homemade soap, it was advisable to rinse well or "the alkali will tell you why."

Leaching the ashes into lye.

From the first settlements until 1825 or so, potash was in great demand in the manufacture of woolen cloth, linen, glass, etc., both here and abroad. It became a prime source of income. As soon as enough people had settled in a township to have a general store, potash was accepted by the storekeeper and credited against the purchase price of pins, needles, tobacco, West India rum, tea and other commodities. Many of the early stores had small buildings in the rear where potash was stored until enough was on hand to be drayed by ox-team or carried by boat to Boston, Albany or Montreal. In some cases the storekeeper took in trade the wood ashes and made the potash himself.

Even if the nearest store was ten or twenty miles distant, potash had the great advantage of being so light in weight, in proportion to its value, that a substantial money's worth could be carried to the store on a man's back, or by a hand sled in winter, to be exchanged for "boughten goods."

In 1791 Vermont produced one thousand tons of potash. Then the roof fell in. In the early 1800s European scientists learned that sodium could be used in place of potash, and be produced from huge salt deposits in Alsace, Germany and Austria. That turned the tide and European potash, or rather its equivalent, was soon being imported into the United States.

[12]

Iron

Gold is for the mistress, silver for the maid,
Copper for the craftsman, cunning at his trade.
"Good" said the Baron, sitting in his hall,
"But Iron, cold Iron, is the master of them all."

—RUDYARD KIPLIN

Despite the magnificence of New England's endless forest, large sections were doomed to be cut down, not to keep the pioneers warm, or to grow their food, or to build houses, barns, bridges and fences, or as material for making potash. The reason was the need for iron. Iron is the fourth most abundant of the elements and comprises five per cent of the earth's crust. A little of it can probably be found in everyone's garden. During thousands of years, iron sometimes collects in the muck and sludge at the bottom of swamps and becomes "bog iron ore."

61

In New England there were no huge deposits of iron ore, such as the Mesabi Range's, in the Lake Superior region, but there were many small ore deposits, close to the surface, such as bog ore as high as twenty-five per cent iron. These deposits often deflected the magnetic needle of the compass so as to cause errors by surveyors in laying out the boundaries of towns.

Within eight years after the landing at Plymouth Rock the pioneers looked for and found some bog iron ore deposits. The ore was assayed and in 1644, at Saugus, Massachusetts, they built the first successful iron smelter on the North American continent. It was one of the wonders of the age. They smelted some of the ore and produced, initially, enough iron to be cast into a small iron pot that would hold about a quart of water! The pot fortunately is still in existence and marks the birth of the most important single industry in America.

Iron ore has to be melted to free the iron contained in it. This melting is done in a smelter where burning charcoal, aided by air (oxygen) from a bellows, develops heat enough to liquify both ore and iron, and thus separates the iron. The heat is about eleven times that of boiling water.

In burning wood in your fireplace a piece of it often gets covered with ashes, but continues to burn slowly without bursting into flames. In the morning

The need for iron.

you have a small piece of black charcoal. It is almost pure carbon. If relighted, and made still hotter by air pumped into the fire by a bellows, you have the secret for obtaining heat hot enough to smelt iron.

The men who burned wood into charcoal had the lonesomest, dirtiest and in many ways the most dangerous job in early New England.

Cords of wood were stacked in mounds up to twenty feet in diameter and five or six feet high. The pile was then carefully covered with wet leaves, weeds and sod, with a small hole at the top as a sort of chimney. The fire had to be controlled to burn slowly without flame. In short, it was to do nothing but smoke for two weeks or more.

The men had to stay on the job night and day, sleeping in miserable bark huts close to the burning mound. It was their responsibility to see that the wood never flamed. If it did, they had to put it out immediately by climbing on the mound and throwing wet sod or snow on it. Men sometimes fell into the burning wood and lost their lives. The charcoal burners were, and are, the forgotten men of the Iron Age. The historians have passed them by.

The demand for wood to make charcoal to smelt the iron created huge "cutovers" in the magnificent forests.

Many iron mines were abandoned, not because they had run out of ore, but because the forest had receded so far from the mine that the cost of bringing charcoal to the smelter became excessive.

The land around Vergennes, Vermont, is an example. Before and during the War of 1812, Vergennes for a short time boasted that it was the iron capital of the United States, with eight forges, a blast furnace and rolling mill. Then the tide moved on to the West where America's huge deposits of coal and iron had been laid down long before either the red man or the white man came. They made coke in place of charcoal. In a few more years the iron industry of New England came to an end. Her forests could grow again.

Wood was used by the pioneers and their descendants to make dozens of useful articles, even wooden clocks. But it seems very doubtful that Europeans would have come and stayed in this new land if they had nothing but stone and wooden implements, clam shells for spades and hoes for planting and weeding corn and pumpkins, and wooden tools for the fireplace.

Freedom to worship God according to conscience is the principal reason given in many of the histories for our ancestors' sailing across the stormy North Atlantic, but American iron kept them from going back.

[13]

Isolation

Man is a gregarious animal and the loneliness of frontier life was a heavy cross to be borne. This was especially true of women. It made many women "queer" and some of them insane. But loneliness was seldom the sole cause. Other factors were overwork, too many babies too close together, too many babies dying, in short, utter weariness of body and soul. There were many families with fifteen or more children. One of the first settlers in Whitingham, Vermont, in 1773, was a man named Pike. He had twenty-eight children, ten by his first wife and eighteen by two others.

66

Isolation

With only trails for roads and walking the only transportation, visits with relatives and friends were difficult and infrequent. Wives often entreated their husbands to move nearer to their relatives and friends, if only during the winter months. A few instances will illustrate how isolated the first-comers were:

The first settlers in Andover, Maine, were Ezekiel Merrill and wife in 1780. "His wife did not see another woman for three years." Abel Stockwell and Francis Whitmore lived in the same Vermont township of Marlboro for nearly a year before either knew of the presence of the other. Benjamin Copp was the first settler in Jackson, New Hampshire, in 1779, and "with his family buffeted the terrors of the wilderness for fourteen years before any other person settled there."

Deacon Aiken settled in Antrim in 1768. No other person moved into the town for the next four years. "He suffered much for want of friends and neighbors."

Isolation was bad enough on the grass-covered prairies of the Mississippi Valley, but there the sun could be seen and its warmth felt. Solitude was worse on the New England frontier which was almost entirely covered by an unending forest of trees, at the feet of which the sun did not penetrate until a clearing had been made. Many of the trees were evergreens that did not shed their leaves in winter.

Many men did not fetch their wives into forest country until they had cleared several acres of land. But the forest was near in any case. Except for the cries of wild animals, the silence was profound, eerie, fear-inspiring. Men and boys on a rock ledge hilltop like to shout and wake the echoes, but in a forest men generally speak in low tones.

Log cabins had tiny openings for windows, but no glass. Rooms were dim in daytime, except for fireplace light. A gloomy atmosphere has some connection with gloomy feelings. Women were indoors more than men.

Just to see, a mile across the valley, the smoke rising from the chimney of a neighbor meant much. Here was help if needed, whether a roof had to be raised or a baby born. Daniel Webster said of the term "the neighbors" that "nobody born in a city knows what the words mean." Except for occasional help from neighbors, it was self-help and self-reliance, a quality greatly valued until recent years. Ralph Waldo Emerson wrote a famous essay on the subject. When self-reliance goes, dependence on others begins.

It is probable that this feeling of self-reliance, of personal independence, of going it alone, if neces-sary, which developed on the New England frontier in the century and a half after Plymouth Rock, had much to do with the Declaration of Independence in 1776.

[14]

Accidents, Sickness, and Death

A pioneer immigrant from Scotland wrote his father and mother in the old country, "My little boy which has Been very unwill these two months he fell in the fire and Burnt one part of his Head."

Fireplaces were on the same level as the cabin floor and required constant watching to keep toddlers and tottering old folks from stumbling into the fire. Sparks were a constant hazard not only to people but to the building itself. They came from both the fireplace and the chimney and sometimes set the roof afire.

Flues often became lined with creosote or wood-tar from the smoke of burning wood. This caused chimney fires which spread to the roof and then to

69

the building itself. When cabins burned to the ground, the ashes were carefully raked to salvage any nails so they could be used again. Except for the nails, a burned cabin was a total loss.

Felling trees was always hazardous even to an expert axe-man. A falling tree was apt to bounce sidewards or kick backwards in unexpected directions when it hit the ground. The husband of the famous Ann Story was one of many who were killed by falling trees.

The father of Robert Rogers, of Rogers' Rangers fame, was mistaken for a bear and was shot and killed. He probably was wearing a greatcoat and hat made of bearskin, which was customary in those days, but dangerous. A four-year-old boy was killed by drinking lye that had been leached from wood ashes.

The son of General Wait of Waitsfield, Vermont, was bitten by a mad dog. The nearest doctor was at Woodstock, forty-four miles away. Rabies or hydrophobia was a terrible hazard in pioneer days as it infected not only dogs but foxes, wolves, skunks and even deer and cattle. The wound from a mad animal's bite was burned by a hot iron, and if this was done quickly enough there was a good chance of avoiding a terrible death. Then there were broken bones, frozen feet, axe cuts, goring by bulls, snake bites, bee stings, drownings and many other accidents.

And nowhere in pioneer country was there such a thing as a completely sterile bandage or a bottle of iodine.

Accidents, Sickness, and Death

The old-timers faced pestilence, consumption, malaria, smallpox, scurvy, spotted fever, cholera and blood poisoning from cuts and accidents. They had no window or door screens, no rubber coats or boots, little or no refrigeration, no central heating or air conditioning. Insects, including the malaria mosquito, swarmed over them and their food day and night. Probably a majority, including the women, went barefoot six months in the year, from frost to frost. They were cold in winter, hot in summer, wet in slush and rain. They worked seventy to eighty hours a week.

Nothing could measure their plight more truly than to say that skilled medical and surgical care was almost totally absent. There were very few doctors, and they were often miles from the man, woman or child who needed them.

"Bleed, puke and purge" was standard practice in the old days. In his last illness on December 12 to 14, 1799, George Washington had, no doubt, the ablest doctors available. He was "bled heavily four times, given gargles of molasses, butter and vinegar, and a blister of cantharides [ground up Spanish flies] was placed on his throat."

Hundreds of Yankee pioneers, men, women and children, had no doubt the same sickness as Washington, with the same result. They had no hospitals, no ambulances, no paved highways, no drug stores, no trained nurses, and no life insurance or social security payable to a widow when her husband died. A widow was almost compelled to remarry to have someone to carry on and help bring up her children.

But mothers in childbirth and small children who died like flies in contagious epidemics needed modern medical care. Their mute gravestones in old cemeteries testify to this.

In a grave in Grafton, Vermont, marked by a famous double headstone, lie the bodies of a young son and thirteen infants, together with the mother who died in 1803. As far as I know, this is the record number of bodies in one grave. Apparently each infant was born dead, and they were buried one after the other in the same grave. The inscriptions on the double stone read as follows:

IN MEMORY OF
THOMAS K. PARK, JUN.
AND THIRTEEN INFANTS
CHILDREN OF
MR. THOMAS K. PARK
AND REBECCA HIS WIFE

Youth behold and
  shed a tear
See fourteen children
  slumber here
See their image how
  they shine
Like flowers of a fruit-
  ful vine

IN MEMORY OF MRS.
REBECCA PARK, WIFE OF
MR. THOMAS K. PARK
WHO DIED SEPT. 23
1803 IN THE 40TH YEAR
OF HER AGE

Behold and see as you
  pass by
My fourteen children
  with me lie
Old and young you soon
  must die
And turn to dust as well
  as I

Hardy, long-lived Revolutionary War veterans.

[15]

Giants in the Earth

Yet, despite sickness and accident, and without our modern aids to health and comfort, the New England pioneers changed a wilderness into a civilization in twenty or thirty years after the first settlements. How were they able to do so much?

One answer is that there was another doctor in the neighborhood, Mother Nature. Her remedies were clean air, sunlight, work, sweat and the pride of free men. Most of the pioneers had elbow grease and the sparkplug of ambition. They were not afraid of work. They were afraid of debt. They had read the Bible and the command from above, "In the sweat of thy face shalt thou eat bread," not the sweat of others.

They did not think they had committed a social sin if their faces and clothes were drenched in sweat. Work did them good and hardship made them tough. Only from struggle comes strength. As Vermont's first historian, Samuel Williams, wrote in 1809, "Temperance and labor do more for them than art and medicine can do for others."

Men and women of today, in contrast to their ancestors, are generally soft and fat. A majority are overweight. They eat too much, drink too much, smoke too much, don't walk enough and drive too fast.

Millions of people now breathe polluted air and drink polluted water made potable only with chlorine or other chemicals. They seldom, if ever, smack their lips over a drink of cool sweet water bubbling from a hillside spring. Their working hours are short, but most of them work indoors under artificial light and under almost constant noise and tension. When not at work they are seldom free from the noise of screeching brakes and honking horns.

This goes by the name of progress. They swallow billions of pills to calm their nerves, put them to sleep and wake them up.

The pioneers worked from sunrise to moon-up, but they went at a slower pace. Their oxen and horses walked only four or five miles an hour. No speed laws were needed. After the forests were cleared, the men spent most of their days in the sunlight and clean fresh air. The women also spent much of the summer working in the sunlight, hanging out the wash and tending the gardens. The noises they heard were mostly the baas of sheep, the moos of cows, the whinny of the old mare, the hum of bees and the music of birdsong.

The old-timers also learned patience and a sense of humor, as this story tells.

For a long time the boundary between Vermont and Massachusetts was unsettled. An old Vermont farmer lived on the land in dispute which his father and grandfather had occupied for eighty years before him. In time a surveying team with their compasses and Gunter chains ran back and forth across the old man's hills and meadows. After a week of this, the surveyors came to the old farmer and told him that a mistake had been made in the old survey. They were awfully sorry to have to tell him that his farm was in Massachusetts. The old man said "nary a word" but kept on shaving fire lighting splinters from a stick of basswood. The young surveyors had expected him to explode.

They said, "It's too bad, grandpa, but it's bully of you to take this sad news so well."

He said, "Don't let it worry you, boys. Fact is, I never did like them Vermont winters none too well, and I'll be glad to live in Massachusetts."

[16]

Patterns

Men and women took great pride in feats of strength and endurance, and in the great age of their ancestors.

George Niles of Shaftsbury, Vermont, lived to be one hundred and five years old. On his hundredth birthday, which came in haying time, his sons, together with their sons, daughters, wives and neighbors came from miles around to do the old man honor. He called his sons "boys," although they were grown men, fifty, sixty, or seventy years old, and experienced farmers themselves. Tradition tells, in substance, how he responded to their good wishes:

"Boys, fetch me a scythe," he said. So they fetched him a scythe.

"Is she whetted good?" the old man asked.

"Just off the grindstone, father. You could shave with it."

The old man took the scythe and felt its razor edge with his thumb. Satisfied, he took the scythe in the crook of his arm and walked out in the meadow where there was a beautiful stand of timothy, or "herd's-grass," as the old-timers called it.

The "boys" followed. And all the neighbors, men and women, children and dogs. The old man had swung a scythe in that meadow for fifty years or more. No one said a word.

The centenarian began to mow. With each swing of the scythe he caught the falling grass on the "heel" of his scythe and deposited it in a beautiful windrow at his left. After going thirty feet or so he stopped. His swath was as straight as a drawn string, every blade of grass cut neat and trim. He was breathing sweet and easy.

"Look thar, boys," he said, "Thar's a pattern for ye!"

Samuel B. Pettengill

Samuel Barrett Pettengill was born in 1886 in Portland, Oregon, where his father was editor of the Portland Oregonian. When he was four years old his mother died and his father brought him to Grafton, Vermont, where his great-grandfather had settled in 1787. He was raised on the old family farm, went to the local one-room school and then to Vermont Academy in Saxtons River, as there was no high school in Grafton. He worked his way through Middlebury College and Yale Law School and then practised law in South Bend, Indiana.

In 1930 he was elected to Congress and became nationally known as a defender of the Constitution and the free enterprise system. After four terms he refused to run again although urged to do so and assured of victory.

He resumed his law practice, wrote a twice-a-week newspaper column for ten years and was a radio commentator for over two years for the American Broadcasting Company on a nationwide hook-up. He was a well-known author and wrote many articles on politics and economics as well as four books, and was renowned as a public speaker.

Mr. Pettengill was an honorary member of the Cum Laude Society of Vermont Academy and was twice awarded the bronze George Washington Honor Medal by Freedoms Foundation of Valley Forge. He belonged to the Sons of the American Revolution, twelve of his ancestors having fought in the Revolutionary War, and he received from the Illinois Society of the S.A.R. their patriotic service award. Five colleges gave him honorary degrees and because of his defense of the Constitution of the United States, he was made a 33rd Degree Mason.

In 1940 he began coming back to Grafton for his vacations and finally retired there in 1956. His last book, THE YANKEE PIONEERS, was written in Grafton as a tribute to his own pioneer ancestors whose courage and self-reliance he had always admired.

Mr. Pettengill was a Director of the Vermont Historical Society and a founder of the Grafton Historical Society, of which he was President for ten years. He died in 1974 and is buried in the Grafton Village Cemetery across the road from his home.

Helen M. Pettengill